The Gift of Hope

The Gift of Hope

BY
ROXIE ANN WESSELS
AND
LISA K. HAM

Beacon Hill Press of Kansas City
Kansas City, Missouri

Copyright 1993
by Beacon Hill Press of Kansas City

First Printing, 1988

New Edition, 1993

Printed in the United States of America
ISBN: 083-411-2256

William A. Rolfe, *Editor*
Amy R. Lofton, *Editorial Assistant*

Cover Design by Crandall Vail
Cover Illustration by Keith Alexander
Illustrations by Ted Ferguson

Note: This book is part of the *Understanding Christian Mission* curriculum. It is designed for use in Year III, Christian Responsibility. This study year examines our responsibility to minister to all the needs of people around the world—physical, mental, emotional, and spiritual. This book was chosen for use in this study year because it shows that when missionaries minister to the needs of people they bring "The Gift of Hope."

10 9 8 7 6 5 4 3 2 1

Contents

1. The Gift of Hope 7
2. Plague! 13
3. Rescued! 22
4. Back from the Dead 31
5. Angry Wind 37

1

The Gift of Hope

by Lisa K. Ham

As the sun peeked over the nearby hills, Joseph felt something tugging at his foot. He opened one eye just enough to see Mother's smile. Carefully the yawning nine-year-old sat up on his straw sleeping mat. His brothers, Henri (on-REE) and Andre (on-DRAY), were snuggled in close on either side. Gently, Joseph slipped out from between them. There was just enough room in the tiny one-room mud house for everyone to lie down. It took some effort to tiptoe around Grandma, Grandpa, three brothers, and three sisters without stepping on anyone.

By the time Joseph had dressed for school Mother had started the charcoal cooking fire outside.

"Hurry, you don't have much time," Mother coaxed.

He grabbed two battered metal pails.

He would have to run to get Mother's water before school. His feet slapped the hard dirt path. Joseph passed by the small, still stream near his house. His family used to get water there. That was before Joseph went to the mission school.

"It would be much easier to get water here. Then I might be able to sleep longer and not yawn so much at school," thought Joseph. "I hate to hurry two miles to the running stream every morning."

But goats and cattle drank and bathed in the still stream. People washed their clothes there too. People at the mission clinic said there were bad things in the water—things you couldn't see with your eyes, called parasites (PAIR-a-sites). They said the water from the still stream had caused much sickness in the village.

At first, Joseph's parents didn't believe the mission health workers. But then they saw that families who got water from the running stream and boiled it didn't get the stomach sickness.

When Joseph was only four years old, two of his

brothers got the stomach sickness. They had died in just a few days. Remembering this made Joseph think it was worth the long trip to get safe water. He also thought he should be the one to make the trip, even though the other children didn't go to school. Though he was not the oldest, Joseph was taller and stronger than his brothers and sisters.

When Joseph reached the running stream, he quickly dipped both buckets into the rushing water and turned for home.

As the sun got brighter, little sweat drops welled up on Joseph's upper lip. He was getting thirsty now. The cool, clear water in the buckets looked delicious. But Joseph decided not to drink any of the water until Mother had boiled it. He did not want to risk getting sick. Joseph couldn't afford to miss even one day of school. There was too much to learn. His family was counting on him to do well. Only a few students would one day graduate and go on to high school in Port-au-Prince. Those who finished high school could get good jobs in the city and buy houses there. Joseph wanted to be one of those graduates. Then he would have his family come live with him, and they would have plenty to eat.

Late one night when everyone else was supposed to be asleep, Joseph had heard Mother and Father talking. Father said the soil was no longer good to farm. "There might not be any rice to harvest, Annette," Father told Mother in a worried tone of voice.

"How are we going to eat?" Joseph wondered, lying there in the darkness. "Even now there is only a little rice, and no money to buy beans."

Since that night, Joseph had decided his hot lunch at school would be his only meal, except for an occasional handful of rice. If he didn't eat at home, there would be more food for the others.

Joseph smiled as he thought of the rumpled photograph in his pocket. He could picture the faces of his Christian sponsor family smiling at him. They sent the mission a gift of money each month to help pay for his school and lunch. Those lunches had helped him grow tall and strong and smart.

Someday Joseph hoped to meet his sponsor family. Their gifts of money meant more than school or food to Joseph. They were gifts of hope—hope for a better future.

When he finally reached home, Joseph stopped just long enough to put down and cover the pails. Then he ran for the schoolhouse. He didn't slow down until he reached the classroom. Huffing and puffing, he plopped down in his seat just in time for the lesson.

The school day went by too quickly for Joseph. He thought about the afternoon's Bible lesson as he walked home. The missionaries said that Jesus was the One who sent them to build the school and clinic. Joseph sensed Jesus was Someone he should learn about, Someone who would be very important to his family.

When he reached the mud house, Grandma and Grandpa were under a shade tree, watching the children. Father hadn't come from the field. "Where are Mother and the baby?" Joseph asked, looking around.

"Inside the house," Grandma answered. "Marie Claude (ma-REE CLODE) may have the stomach sickness."

Inside Mother was getting Marie Claude ready for a trip to the mission clinic. Mother was very glad to see Joseph.

"Joseph, I need you to make the special drink you learned about in school for your sister," Mother said. "She has been very sick today."

Joseph rushed outside to the lime tree. He picked one small lime and ran back to the house. He filled a cup from the buckets of boiled water and squeezed the lime into it. Then he added a pinch of salt and sugar. After stirring the mixture, he handed the cup to Mother.

Propped on Mother's lap, Marie Claude drank the cup dry. She gave Joseph a faint smile, and then snuggled in close to Mother.

"Thank you, Joseph! You are such a help to us. Now help me get Marie to the clinic," Mother said. "She will be fine if we can see the nurse right away."

2

Plague!

by Roxie Ann Wessels

Many nine-year-old Indian girls worked the fields with their mothers, but Shanti (shawn-tee) stayed at home. She had to take care of her younger brother, Chubi (chew-bee), and a little neighbor girl, Usha (oo-sha).

The day had been long and tiring for Shanti. Chubi had been cross. He had cried most of the day. There were times when Shanti wanted to spank him to make him be quiet. But she didn't.

"Usha, I know why Chubi is cross," Shanti said. "It's that terrible sore on his stomach."

"What makes the sore?" Usha asked.

"Two weeks ago Chubi had a bad stomachache. The village healer came. But his mixture of herbs and magic could not stop the ache," Shanti told her. "So he burned Chubi's stomach to let the evil spirit out."

"Poor little Chubi!" Shanti said.

Besides caring for Chubi and Usha, Shanti also cleaned the house. That day she had swept the sun-baked floor with a twig broom. She had rolled up the children's grass sleeping mats and carried Mother and Father's sleeping cots into the courtyard. Usha had helped her polish the brass plates and cups.

"I must hurry and get supper ready," Shanti told Usha. "My parents will be home soon."

In one corner of the room stood a stove made of hard baked mud. It would burn wood, but now most of the trees were gone. No one used wood in their stoves any more. Every day the girls went out to find cow dung. They rolled it in balls to burn.

Using dried dung balls as fuel, Shanti started the cooking fire. The house filled with smoke.

From brown wheat dough, she pinched off a small ball, flattened it with her fingers, then tossed it back and forth until it was thin and round. Finally Shanti baked the *chapatties* (cha-pa-tees) on an iron *tawa* (taa-waa) plate over the fire.

"Please put the milk, sugar and tea leaves in the kettle, Usha," Shanti said.

The sun was now sinking behind the hills. Shanti looked through the window bars. She could see some people coming.

"Here they come. Run, Usha, run!"

Usha ran out into the street to join her parents for their walk home.

Chubi stretched out his arms to his mother

"You thin, little pheasant," she teased. "We've got to get some flesh on these bones!"

Father's pants were covered with dirt, as were his face, hands, and feet. But that didn't keep him from enjoying Shanti's supper. Seated cross-legged on the floor he ate alone.

While Father ate, Mother fed the baby. Then Shanti and her mother enjoyed what was left of the rice and gravy, chapatties, and tea. Mother patted Shanti's back. "My little girl does the work of a woman. You are a good daughter. The gods will favor you. Now have a good sleep," she said.

Shanti unrolled her grass mat in the corner. Soon she was fast asleep.

Chubi's crying awakened Shanti in the middle of the night. She sat up and rubbed her eyes. Lamp light flickered dimly across the room. She could see Mother holding Chubi.

"He's sick again," Mother told Father. "He is so hot; he must have the fever."

Shanti knew fever usually meant death.

By morning Chubi was much worse. Father ran for the village healer.

Shanti didn't like the healer. He wore a loincloth about his waist and a turban on his head. He carried two jars filled with some mixture. It smelled so bad Shanti had to hold her nose. She feared the strange charms hanging around his neck.

The healer forced Chubi to drink some of the "smelly" mixture. "That is my special medicine," he muttered. "Now we must drive out the evil spirit. Put the boy on the floor and make him jump up and down."

"But my son is only one," Chubi's mother objected. "And he's too sick to jump up and down."

"Then we must make a sacrifice to the gods. Bring me a goat," he ordered.

Chubi's parents looked at each other. "Our only goat was stolen," they said sadly.

"Then the boy will die," the village healer said. He picked up his jars and started to leave. "Now you must pay me!"

Father took a small tin box from under a ragged quilt. He emptied four silver coins into the healer's hand.

After the healer had gone, Chubi's parents began to weep. "O Krishna (krish-na), Rama (ra-ma), all the gods, have mercy. Help us now!"

Chubi died that day.

That evening there was no supper. Shanti and her parents didn't feel like eating. They didn't feel like talking.

"I shall not go to the field tomorrow," Mother said. "Chubi's death has broken my heart."

"All right," Father said. "Shanti can take your place in the field tomorrow."

The early morning sun awoke Shanti. "Today I help Father," she remembered. She got up quickly.

"Where's Father? Did he leave without me?" she wondered.

Her mother had not gotten up. Something was wrong. Shanti ran to her mother's cot.

"What is it, Mother? What is wrong?" Her mother's face looked swollen. Her breathing was short.

"Listen to me, Shanti. Promise you will be brave. Now I am sick. I will die soon. I have tried to do good deeds. I've offered sacrifices and fasted. Perhaps I will

17

be reborn into a better life. Pray to the god Siva (shee-va). He can do this for me."

"Please don't leave me!" Shanti cried. "Take me with you."

"No, my child. Your father has gone for the missionary doctor many miles away. Go now. You must work in the field today. Usha's father will show you what to do."

Two days later Shanti's father returned with the missionary doctor But it was too late! Shanti's mother had died.

The doctor looked very worried. She asked Shanti's father many questions. "Have you seen any rats?"

Father nodded "Yes."

Fear crossed the doctor's face. "It's the plague!"

she told her helpers. "If we don't act quickly, many will die!"

They got busy at once. First the doctor gave Shanti a shot. One man dusted insect killer all over the house—every nook, crack, and corner.

The other helper hunted for rats and their holes. "Here's where a rat was living—here under the wall of the courtyard," he cried. He sprayed poison into the hole with a small hand pump. Then he covered it over with mud to be sure fleas carrying the disease could not come out.

The terrible disease had spread through the village more than Father or Shanti had realized. Several were sick. Many were so frightened they piled their belongings into oxcarts and went to live in the fields.

The missionary explained that Shanti's vaccine would keep her from getting sick. The doctor would vaccinate everyone in the village. But getting the people to take a shot was difficult. Children were frightened at the sight of a needle. Parents and grandparents were scared too. Many of them hid under their cots. The helpers had to drag them from their hiding places so the doctor could give the shots. Often at night the doctor and helpers went through the houses giving shots to those who had escaped during the day.

Every home had to be fumigated and cleaned. The helpers sprayed clothing, mats, boxes—everything in the homes—with insect killer. The disease-carrying rats had to be destroyed, their holes sprayed with poison, and the openings sealed shut.

The doctor and her helpers worked day and night to save the village! By the time the disease was under control, 40 villagers had died. Shanti lost both her parents. Father died the first week after the doctor came. Usha's parents died too.

"Your father was brave, Shanti," said the missionary doctor. "If he hadn't come for me, many more of your people would have died. You can always be proud of him."

Shanti *was* proud. Yet she felt very lonely. "Usha has an uncle and aunt. I have no one now," she thought.

"Shanti, would you like to come live with me?" the doctor said as she prepared to leave. "You could help me, and go to the mission school."

Shanti ran into her arms. She was crying and laughing all at once.

"Oh. I would love it! I would love it!"

* * *

Shanti adjusted quickly to life in her new home. She helped with the housework, the meals, and the garden. She was very quick to learn to read and write. She soon decided that she would be a nurse.

"But I will be a Christian nurse," she said. "I want to live for Jesus, as you have."

After seven years of study and work Shanti became a Christian nurse. One day the head nurse of the children's ward spoke to her.

"Shanti, I need your help. A Hindu girl was brought into the hospital yesterday. Her condition is serious. She has been sick for more than a year. She is afraid of all the missionary nurses and doctors.

"She can't remember her parents. They died when she was only three. Her uncle and aunt raised her."

Shanti hurried to the children's ward. She found a

frightened, wide-eyed girl staring at the ceiling. Something seemed strangely familiar about the girl on the bed. But Shanti wasn't sure what it was.

"Hello," Shanti said as she looked at the record card taped on the head of the bed.

"I see on your card that you are from my old village. I lived there until I was nine. In fact I used to know a little girl with your name, Usha. She lived next door and I took care of her. How old are you?"

"Ten!" came Usha's faint answer.

Shanti's heart beat faster Could this be the little Usha she used to know? She looked deeply into the 10-year-old's eyes. Suddenly she was sure.

Shanti took Usha's hands in hers. "You are my little Usha. And I am going to take care of you again. Jesus is going to help you to get well, you will see."

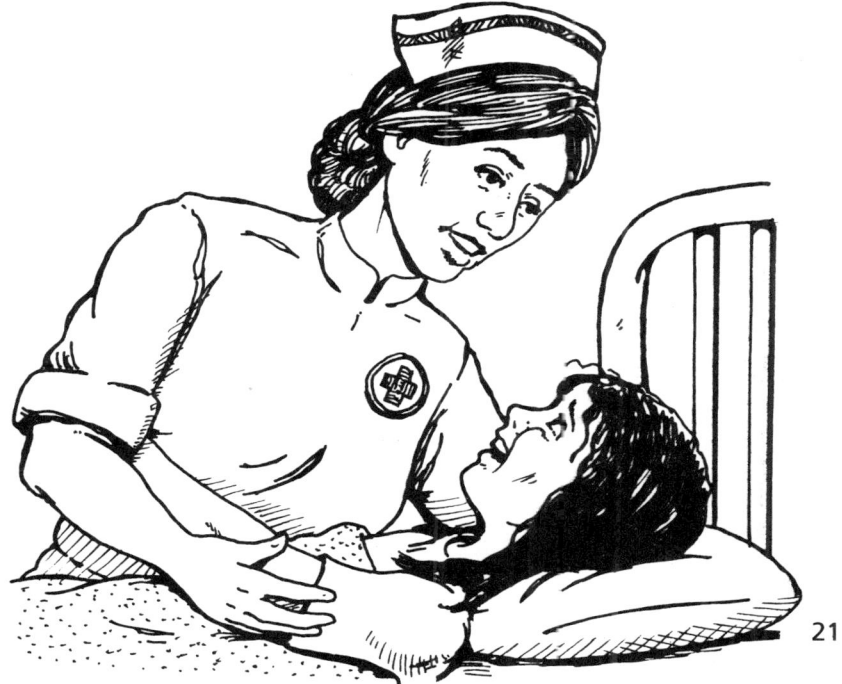

3

Rescued!

by Roxie Ann Wessels

"One Horn isn't with the rest of the cows," Hopi (HOPE-ee) said to Musa (MUSE-ah), his older brother. The two boys were sitting under a clump of thorn trees.

"Well, go find her," Musa said, without looking up.

Hopi frowned but didn't answer. He knew what to do without being told. Musa was 14 and liked to boss his 10-year-old brother

"Musa isn't helping at all today," Hopi thought as he walked to the stream looking for One Horn. "I have to do all the work."

It was true. The older boys played or loafed while the younger boys worked. The younger ones knew not to complain or they would be punished. It was all a part of their training.

The missing cow was not far away. Hopi soon had her back with the herd. He sat down near Musa and began to draw a picture in the sandy soil.

"Do you think Father will let me go, Musa?" he asked. He stood up to look at his picture.

"Go where, silly?" said Musa.

"To Vacation Bible School at the mission. Haven't you heard? It's just for two weeks. And I'd be gone for only three hours in the mornings. Musa, I want to go more than anything!"

"Well, don't get so excited. If I promised Father to do your herding for you, maybe you could go." Musa tried to sound older than 14.

"Come on now; the sun is setting. It's time to go home." Musa kicked the dirt over Hopi's picture and got up.

Hopi gathered the cows and started home. Musa soon caught up.

Musa ran ahead while Hopi shut the cows in their pen. By the time Hopi joined the family in the yard, Musa had already told Father about Hopi's wish to go to Vacation Bible School.

"Let Hopi tell me what he wants to do," said Father

So Hopi began to tell of the school. "I will work extra hard when I'm home. And Musa said he will herd the cows for me for the two weeks. May I go, Father?" Hopi pleaded.

"Well, Musa, if you will watch the cows for Hopi, he can go," said Father.

Hopi grinned.

※ ※ ※

Hopi was the first to arrive at VBS, so the missionary teacher let him ring the bell. Children came from every direction.

"Come sit with me," Hopi invited Bangu (BANG-goo), an 11-year-old boy from a kraal (KRAWL) nearby.

Bangu looked unhappy. His older brother, the witch doctor, had made him come. He wanted Bangu to find out the "magic" of the missionary teacher.

Bangu jumped over two logs to sit by Hopi.

That morning they sang new songs. Then the missionary teacher used a big board and pictures to tell a

Bible story. Later they ran races and wove baskets in the shade.

"What's wrong, Bangu?" Hopi asked.

"I don't like to weave. And I'm not going to!" Bangu snapped.

"Bangu must be angry all the time. Or maybe he is afraid," thought Hopi. "If my brother were a witch doctor, I'd be scared too."

The dismissal bell rang and the children ran home. They could hardly wait until the next day.

On Friday, Hopi couldn't find Bangu.

"Do you know where Bangu is?" the teacher asked.

"I haven't seen him," Hopi said. "But I'll go look for him."

Hopi first thought of the river! When he came to the riverbank he pulled back the bushes for a peek. Lying on the bank on one side was an old log covered with bushes and weeds.

Nearby was another log. Standing on top was Bangu. He'd gone swimming.

Bangu didn't hear Hopi come through the bushes. He almost fell off the log when Hopi spoke.

"Having fun?" Hopi asked. Before he could say more Bangu waved and jumped into the river again.

"Why don't you come in? This is fun," said Bangu.

Hopi was tempted but he answered, "I don't want to miss out on Bible school. Come on, Bangu."

Hopi glanced over at the log covered with weeds. Under the weeds he saw an eye open and stare at him. Hopi shivered from head to foot.

"It's no log at all," thought Hopi. "Look, Bangu, a crocodile!"

The eye opened again.
"Bangu, get out! He is waking up. Get out!"
Bangu didn't have to be told again. His dark eyes

grew large. His body trembled. The crocodile moved toward Bangu.

Hopi knew he would have to get the crocodile's attention away from Bangu. He yelled at the crocodile. When it came closer he pushed a log toward it so Bangu would have time to climb out.

Bangu's escape made the crocodile very angry. He snorted and thrashed his tail. When the powerful tail hit the log Hopi was pushing, the impact broke Hopi's arm. Hopi shrieked, and the old crocodile glided down river for a quieter spot.

"My arm, my arm!" cried Hopi. He tried to lift it with his other hand. Pain shot through his body.

Quickly, Bangu helped Hopi through the bushes.

Hopi moaned with pain. He asked to sit and rest under the tree. He felt weak in the knees and sick to his stomach.

"I'll run and get my brother,' suggested Bangu. "He can help."

"Has your brother ever made a crooked arm straight?" Hopi asked. "No, I don't want him to come. I want to see the missionary teacher. She can help."

"I will not go with you, Hopi. The teacher will blame me for your broken arm. She will put a curse on me!" Bangu's voice was very loud. "I will go now for my brother."

"Please stay with me, Bangu," begged Hopi. "I need you. It's a long way back to Bible school!" But Bangu was already gone.

Hopi struggled up and turned toward the church. But his head began to go round and round. He felt faint.

"In a few minutes I can go on," he said to himself. He closed his eyes to stop the tears.

In the meantime Bangu spread the news of the crocodile. The men of his kraal grabbed spears and clubs and ran to the river to kill it.

Bangu found his brother and told him about Hopi's accident.

The next time Hopi opened his eyes, he saw Bangu and his brother, the witch doctor. The witch doctor was bending over a bag of medicine on the ground.

He wore a grass skirt and a headdress of long red and white feathers. There were circles of red and white paint around his eyes. About his neck and ankles dangled bracelets of bones and horns.

"Has your father made offerings to the demons lately?" he muttered.

Hopi did not answer. He was in too much pain.

"Boy, the evil spirits are angry with you and your father. Here, drink this medicine I have made." The witch doctor tried to force Hopi's mouth open.

Hopi refused.

"Bangu, I saved your life. Please take me to the missionary teacher. She can make my arm well." Hopi was crying.

Bangu turned his head. He could not bear to watch Hopi in pain. He felt sorry for Hopi, and guilty too.

"I am going to have to build a fire and burn your arm. That will drive the evil spirits from you," mumbled the witch doctor.

"Please, don't!" begged Hopi. "Wait! I see someone coming this way."

Never had Hopi seen a more beautiful sight! It was the missionary teacher and two of the older boys from the school. They had been looking everywhere for Bangu and Hopi.

The witch doctor scowled angrily. "Go away! Go away!" he ordered. "The spirits are angry, and we must calm them." He began to mutter over his medicine.

Hopi looked hopeful as the missionary came toward him. He was no longer frightened of the witch doctor.

Although his legs were trembling, Hopi tried to stand and walk to the teacher. "I don't want your medicine," he told the witch doctor. "I'm going to the missionary doctor. He can stop the pain and make my arm straight again."

The witch doctor gave a loud yell and picked up his medicine bag to leave.

The two older boys made a seat of their arms and, with the missionary's help, carried Hopi back to the mission clinic.

Hopi's arm was set and put in a cast. Every day the missionary teacher came to see him. She told him about Jesus and His love for all boys and girls. She told him how he could become a Christian. They prayed together. Hopi told God the bad things he had done. He asked God to forgive him and make him a Christian.

Hopi attended the last morning of Vacation Bible School. He could not play or work with his hands, but he could listen and sing songs. Bangu was there too.

"I like being here with you, Hopi," Bangu said. "You are a good friend to me. And I have learned something about the mission people from you."

"What have you learned?" Hopi asked eagerly.

"I have seen them make your arm better and take away your pain," said Bangu. "Others have seen too. There is talk that the missionary's medicine must be better than the witch doctor's. Even my brother has seen."

"Have you also seen that the Christians really care about us and our families?" Hopi asked anxiously.

"Yes," replied Bangu with a smile. "I don't understand everything . . . but I see something good."

4

Back from the Dead

by Roxie Ann Wessels

One rainy afternoon Ina and her mother made their way through the New Guinea jungle to the bush church. This was the first time Ina had gone to the weekly class for women and girls. She was going to learn to sew!

Mrs. Wilson, the missionary, asked if Ina would like to join the class. Ina eagerly answered, "Yes." Mrs. Wilson gave her a piece of material, thread, and a needle.

Ina sat cross-legged on the bamboo floor of the church. She tried to make the needle go in and out in a straight line. But the thread always became tangled. It seemed so hard! Her mother, Lun, had to help her. Finally Lun had to finish Ina's sewing for her.

Later that afternoon Ina listened carefully to the Bible story. She tried to sing the songs about Jesus. As months passed, Ina and her mother learned more and more about Jesus. Mrs. Wilson said Jesus wanted to be Ina's friend.

One morning Mrs. Wilson asked, "Is there anyone who would like to live for Jesus?"

Ina raised one finger right in front of her face. She opened one eye to see if anyone was looking. Two others besides Ina had raised their hands. One was Lun, Ina's mother.

Mrs. Wilson explained that Jesus had come to show God's love. He had made it possible for God to forgive everyone's sins—things they did to disobey God.

Ina wanted God to forgive her. She prayed and told Him she was sorry for the wrong things she had done. She was glad He forgave her.

Weeks passed but Ina didn't come back to the sewing meeting. One time her mother came and said Ina was sick.

The next week Lun didn't come. The other women told Mrs. Wilson that Ina was very sick! Lun had to stay home.

Soon after the class, Mrs. Wilson and her interpreter went back into the bush to visit Ina. They had to leave the jeep at the bush church. The trail led through thick branches and vines, over fences, and across cold mountain streams.

Finally they reached the house where Ina, her mother, and sisters lived with the other women and girls. Sitting around outside on the ground were Ina's father, uncles, cousins, and friends. They were all crying and moaning. They were sure Ina would die!

Poor Ina! She lay unconscious on a pile of leaves, her head in her mother's lap.

"She looks so different from the little girl we saw

in church a few weeks ago!" the missionary said to the interpreter.

"She certainly looks near death to me," answered the interpreter.

Mrs. Wilson walked up to the father and asked, "May we have permission to pray?"

"*Ee-got, ee-got*" ("yes, yes"), said the father.

When she finished her prayer Mrs. Wilson spoke to Ina's father.

"Ina should go to the dispensary at the mission in the valley She is hot with fever."

"That is too far away from our own ground. If she dies, she must die here. If she dies on strange ground, her spirit will haunt us all," the father answered.

"But maybe she will *not* die," the missionary said. "If she gets good, strong medicine, she may live. But she *will* die if she stays here!"

"Who will take care of Ina while she is in the hospital?" questioned her father. "Her mother cannot go. She has to stay here and take care of the pigs."

"Can't another woman take care of the pigs this time? Your little girl is dying!" the missionary pleaded.

The father made more excuses. "Our garden has been poor, and we have no food to take with us. We will all starve in the valley."

"The mission has gardens. And we have food at the dispensary for those who come from far away," said the missionary.

Ina's mother had stopped crying. She turned to her husband and said, "I believe God is strong and good. I believe He will help Ina if we take her to the mission hospital and get the medicine for her."

The husband stared at her. It was unusual for a New Guinea woman to speak up so openly. The father hesitated. "I guess we will go," he said at last.

He picked up the almost lifeless child and, holding on to her thin arms, carried her on his back. Lun hurriedly grabbed her string-bag and a few bananas and followed. The whole family went with the little group back over the trail to the church. They cried and wailed as they walked, because they thought they would never see Ina well again.

Back at the church, the missionary directed the mother and the father to the jeep. They had never been inside a thing like that before. Both trembled and stepped back. They were terrified.

"That machine will kill us," said the father. "We cannot go."

"l will make the jeep go very, very slowly. I will see to it that it does not kill us," the missionary promised.

Both parents cautiously climbed into the back of the jeep. They sat on the floor with their eyes closed, clutching each other and crying. The jeep crept slowly down the steep mountain road to the mission station in the valley.

The nurse examined Ina the minute her father carried her inside. She could see Ina had malaria. If she recovered, the missionary and nurse could not promise she would be completely normal again.

Ina was kept warm and dry in the dispensary as she slept and rested. At last the medicines began to help. The missionary visited her every day. She also told Ina and her parents about God and His great love for them.

"God is helping Ina get well," the missionary said.

The next week when the missionary and the interpreter went back to the bush church for the meeting, they found many people already there. The people were covered with mud and were mourning and wailing.

"Who has died?" Mrs. Wilson asked.

"We are crying for Ina. We know she must be dead," they said.

The missionary quickly replied, "Ina is not dead. She is getting better in the hospital."

The people continued to cry. "We hear, but we cannot believe you. We know we will never see her again."

But Ina *did* get well!

Five weeks later she left the dispensary. She and her mother rode in the jeep with the missionary back to the little bush church. Again a group of people waited for the meeting to begin. When they saw Ina and her mother step out of the jeep, they ran screaming to meet them.

"It is really Ina!" they cried. They hugged her and felt her to see if she was real.

"It is as if she were dead and has come back again to us. What Lun said must be true. 'God is strong and good.' Surely He has helped Ina!"

5

Angry Wind

by Lisa K. Ham

"What's wrong, Roel (roe-EL)?" Miraflor (MEAR-a-floor) Detalo (de-TALL-oh) asked her oldest brother. "You look so serious, and you're running around like a nervous chicken."

"I don't like this weather," Roel answered. He crawled to the opening of their makeshift house to take another look outside. "The rain isn't going to let up."

"What do you expect, silly?" Miraflor responded. "That's why this is called the 'rainy season.'"

"But listen," Roel argued. "It's coming down much harder, and the wind is picking up."

Miraflor stopped stirring the pot of boiling rice long enough to listen to the rain pounding the tin roof. "It sounds like hundreds of hammers," Miraflor said anxiously. Then she reached to pull her little sister, Martina (mar-TEE-na), closer. "Are you afraid, Roel?" she asked. "Do you think . . ."

"Shhhh!" Roel cautioned her. "Listen!"

Roel and Miraflor heard a loudspeaker and the sound of army trucks. They were driving across the crest of the steep hill overlooking the beach on which Roel's family and hundreds of others made their homes.

"EVACUATE!" a gruff voice said. "TYPHOON!"

The word sent chills down Roel's back. He stood stunned. He was unable to move until a strong gust of wind knocked him to the ground. Scrambling to his feet, Roel struggled into the house. His sister had wrapped a thin blanket around Martina. "Roenna (roe-EE-na)!

"Eleazer (el-ee-AY-zer)!" she shouted. "Hurry! We're leaving NOW!"

The thin walls of the tiny house began to rattle.

Everything was happening at once. Roel couldn't think. He wished Mother and Father were here instead of at work.

His thoughts were interrupted by a shrill scream from somewhere outside the house.

"NATHAN!" Miraflor shrieked. "He is outside by himself!"

Roel ran outside to find his eight-year-old brother wrapped around the remains of a tiny tree. "Help me!" Nathan screamed.

Roel strained to put one foot in front of the other toward Nathan. He walked as though he were climbing an invisible ladder. He had almost reached the tree when a large metal sheet from the roof of a nearby house struck Roel and knocked him to the ground. When the wind would not let him up, he crawled to Nathan.

The frail little boy was frightened by all the noise, the screams, the falling trees and houses. He sobbed fiercely in Roel's arms.

Miraflor and the other children made their way from the house to a nearby tree. "Where do we go?" Miraflor called out. "The soldiers said to go to higher ground."

Roel could hardly hear his sister's voice, though she was just a few feet away. The angry wind nearly swallowed her words.

"Just climb!" Roel shouted. He reached out an arm to Miraflor while he held Nathan and the tree with the other.

With great effort, the children huddled around the flimsy tree. "Hang on!" Roel shouted as he started up the hillside.

The wind pulled and pushed the children in every direction. They clung to fallen trees, stones, and the remains of houses for support as they slowly made their way up the hill.

By now the rain came down so hard they could hardly see. The raindrops felt like rocks.

"There!" Roel shouted, pointing to a high concrete wall near the top of the hill. "Get behind it!"

Miraflor could barely see where Roel pointed. Little Martina screamed all the louder as Miraflor tightened her arms around the baby. Eleazer and Roenna had their arms locked around Roel's waist, while Nathan clung to his back.

When Roel slipped in the mud, Miraflor reached out to help him. As he struggled to his feet, Miraflor realized her other arm was empty. Martina was gone!

"Roel!" Miraflor screamed. "The baby!"

"Come on!" Roel shouted. He could not hear or see what had happened. "We're almost there!"

By the time the children sank behind the security of the wall, their strength was gone. They were too tired to move, too tired to talk, and too tired to cry. They huddled together in a little wet heap. The wind and rain raged around and below them. All along the bottom of the hill, houses and people and animals were being washed from the hillside by an angry wall of water.

The next time Roel opened his eyes, he saw a clear sky. He closed his eyes and opened them again slowly. He hoped to find the storm had been a horrible nightmare.

Lying next to him, Miraflor had Nathan wrapped tightly in her arms. Eleazer and Roenna were huddled together at Roel's feet. Roenna's eyes were open. But she was not moving, only staring out into nothing.

Roel wrapped himself around her to keep her warm.

All along the wall, bodies were huddled together in wet piles.

Suddenly Miraflor awoke screaming for her lost

sister. It was then Roel realized Martina was gone. Miraflor flung herself into the safety of her brother's arms. Roel stroked her stringy wet hair and held her tightly as she sobbed. Her cries awoke Nathan and Eleazer. They crawled into the huddle to cry too.

Roel wondered about his parents. Had the city survived the typhoon? "Lord, please help us find them," he whispered.

Then he felt a warm hand on his shoulder and looked up into the eyes of Pastor Joel Galgo (GAWL-go). Comforted by a friendly face, Roel released a flood of tears and wrapped an arm around his pastor's neck. He had never cried so hard before.

"Praise be to God!" Pastor Galgo repeated over and over. "I knew the Lord would lead me to you!"

"Our parents?" Roel interrupted. "Do you know . . ."

"Yes," assured the pastor. "They are alive. Your father rode his peddle cab to my house just as the storm blew in. We went together to find your mother."

"Is Mother all right?" Miraflor asked, wiping at her tears.

"Yes, she's at the mission clinic,' the pastor answered. "The sewing factory collapsed in the storm. But your mother got out in time. She has only a few cuts and bruises. The nurse at the mission says she will be fine."

"Have you seen Martina?" Miraflor asked hopefully.

"No," her pastor said slowly. "I was hoping she was with you."

"She was . . ." Miraflor sobbed, "until I lost her climbing the hill."

"We can pray that one of the rescue workers will find her," Pastor Galgo said. Then he gave Miraflor a reassuring smile. "We're to meet your parents at the mission house. Can you walk?"

Roel and Miraflor struggled to their feet. Roel lifted Nathan into his arms. Roenna was still staring off in space. Pastor Galgo carried her while Eleazer tagged along behind him.

Everywhere buildings, trees, animals, and people lay in crumpled wet piles. Survivors were busy searching for food and belongings under the fallen trees and houses.

Slowly the tiny caravan made their way to an old pickup truck on the hillside. Roel's eyes met the sad, frightened stares of eight strangers as he climbed into the truck bed.

With the children safely in the truck, Pastor Galgo motioned the driver. Then he flashed the children a smile. "Glen will take you to the mission," he said. "I'm going to see what we can do here. Then I'll be right behind you."

"I'm Ebenezer (eb-en-EE-zer) Valdez (val-DEZ)," said the boy next to Roel. "They say my father is at this place we are going. Are your parents there too?"

"Yes," Roel answered.

"Do you know this place?" Ebenezer looked uneasy.

"The missionaries are close friends of my father's," Roel answered. "They told us of Pastor Galgo and his church. The Christians are kind people, Ebenezer. You don't have to worry."

"My mother is dead," Ebenezer went on. "I have not seen any of my brothers and sisters since the storm. Our home is gone . . ." Ebenezer lowered his head and cried.

Thinking of Martina, Roel put an arm around Ebenezer and cried too. A year before he had lost a brother and sister to the typhoon. "Why does this keep happening to us?" he questioned. "Why, God?" Tears streamed down his face as the truck bumped along the worn road to the mission.

"Daddy!" Nathan screamed as the truck reached the mission yard. Roel had to grab Nathan's T-shirt to keep him from flying out of the truck before it stopped. When Roel let go, Nathan leaped into his father's arms. When all his children had gotten off the truck, Elmer Detalo gave each one a hug and a kiss and then asked them to bow for a prayer.

"Gracious Father, thank You for bringing my children and for saving their mother. Take care of my little one, Lord. I know You will. In Jesus' name . . . Amen."

"How can you thank God after what He has done to us!" Roel shouted unexpectedly. He covered his eyes and turned to run away.

Father, sent the other children to their mother and went to find Roel. He found him crying in an old shed outside the mission clinic.

"Why do you blame God for what happened, Roel?" Father asked softly. "Do you think He wants to hurt us?"

"Yes, Father, I do!" Roel answered. "Pastor Galgo says the Lord loves us. But how could He do this if that is true?"

"Roel," Father began, "God did not force us to live on that dangerous hillside. People do that to us—those who have land in the safe mainland but do not want to share it with others. It is people who make us work hard all day and pay us so little money that we can barely feed ourselves and only dream of buying safe land for our home."

"Then why doesn't God *help* us find a safe home?"

45

Roel asked. "He has seen what the storms do to people. Why doesn't He help us?"

"Oh, but He has, Roel!" Father interrupted. "Come with me. I want to share some good news."

Roel wiped his eyes. They walked into the mission and found Mother and the children eating a hot lunch.

"This afternoon," Father began, "I spoke with Glen about our family. My friend asked if we would like to build our new house here in the hills. Our church will help us buy the land and make a strong cement house that will be safe in the storms."

Roel looked up in amazement. The other children clapped and cheered.

"Wait," Father interrupted. "There is more! The other missionaries asked me to send you to the mission school. Would you like that?"

Roel didn't know what to say. He felt ashamed for the way he had acted. Roel had dreamed of graduating from school and getting a good job in the city. With the money he could earn, his family could eat well every day.

Roel's thoughts were interrupted by Pastor Galgo. He asked to speak to Father alone. They left the room together.

When Father returned, he whispered to Mother. She nodded. Then Father motioned to Roel. He had a sad look on his face.

"Roel," he said. "Pastor has told me Mr. Valdez is dead. The nurses could not stop his bleeding. His son, Ebenezer, was the only one in his family to survive. Now he is all alone."

"I met Ebenezer on the truck coming here," Roel added. "What will he do now?"

"Remember what I have told you that helping each other is God's plan for us?" Father asked. "I have told Pastor that Ebenezer can live with us, if he wants to."

"Did you ask him?" Roel asked thoughtfully.

"I was hoping *you* would ask him, Roel. You're the same age. And you've already met."

"I'll go find him, Dad," Roel said.

Roel found Ebenezer huddled by the front porch steps. Ebenezer saw Roel coming and quickly wiped his tears.

"I have come to ask you something," Roel began.

Ebenezer looked up but didn't speak.

"My father told me about your family," said Roel.

"He sent me to ask you if you want to come and live with us."

Ebenezer only stared at Roel.

"I think you will like my family," Roel stammered on. "I know it's not the same as your *own* family."

A tiny tear started down Ebenezer's cheek.

"But I can promise you that this will not happen to us again. My father says we are going to have a strong house here in the hills. And you and I will go to school!"

Ebenezer could not speak. He only stared at Roel in amazement.

Roel took his hand and led him toward the mission house. "Things will be different for us now," Roel comforted. "You'll see."